Collage Quilter

Essentials for Success with Collage Quilts

| 2nd Edition |

Emily Taylor

Dedicated to my family~
Joe, Amelia, Caroline and Harrison

Acknowledgments

My dear friend, Quinn Silcox, has nurtured me along in the dark days and has cheered my success in the bright days.

Kaffe Fassett, Phillip Jacobs, Anna Maria Horner and others, who inspire my work with their gorgeous color palettes and designs.

Marion McClellan is a gem of a human and a genius with a long-arm machine! I am ever appreciative for her artistry and professionalism in quilting my projects.

Photographer Rachael Hodson, another amazing human assisted me with shots used in this book. Find her at @ rachaelhodsonphoto on Instagram.

Finally, I have incredible gratitude for my husband, Joe, who has mastered the patience required to live with a fiercely passionate, ambitious and sometimes ill-tempered creator.

CONTENTS

INTRODUCTION

A collage quilt is a unique form of fiber art~ one that closely mimics a painting in the process by which it's made and in how it looks. Like painting, a collage quilt is created by understanding and applying the principles of color, value, temperature and contrast to the process of fabric selection and fabric application. While a traditional quilt requires rigid adherence to fabric quantities and sewing methods, in collage quilt-making the fabric quantities are fluid and there are no strict measurements for cutting or piecing.

My method for creating a collage quilt is achieved by overlapping small fabric pieces with adhesive to create a design. The edges of each fabric piece are left raw. The methods taught in this book provide for the greatest freedom of expression and creativity with fabric and the result is that every collage quilt (even one made by following a pattern) is absolutely unique and impossible to replicate.

As I have been working to refine my own techniques and train my eye to see nuances in a wide variety of fabric, I have fallen even more deeply in love with this medium! The challenge of finding the right fabric for each piece is exhilarating and I am passionate about my craft. I consider myself to be at the nascent of my career as a collage quilter, and the more collage quilts I create, the more I realize the depth of this form of artistic expression. There is nothing that pacifies my need to create quite like losing myself in the work of a collage quilt. I hope with this book to share the principles for success that I'm learning along my artistic journey!

~Emily

1
COLOR THEORY

Color makes things exciting! Color elicits an emotional response in us. When we understand the power that color has, we can be more effective wielding it as a tool in our collage quilts!

Just as a traditional artist seeks to understand and implement principles of art, so should we as collage quilters. The only difference is our choice of medium-- rather than using paint, we are using fabric. A collage quilt is a form of art quilt and the quality of our finished project is elevated when we have a good grasp of color theory.

I like to think of collage quilts as a form of Impressionism. One of the important distinctions of the Impressionist masters like Monet, Degas, Manet, and Renoir from other schools of art is the way they applied paint to a canvas. Their method was to load a brush with paint and apply it to the canvas. Then they would do it again. And again. There was not much effort made to smooth and blend the brushstrokes. Rather, the application of color provided the blending of surrounding brushstrokes. Our application of fabric is much the same. It is through the precise selection and placement of fabric (based on our understanding of color theory), that we can create an artistic collage quilt.

Additionally, collage quilts are similar to Impressionism in their painterly appearance and imperfection. When an Impressionist painting is viewed up close, it can be difficult to discern the subject of the composition. In fact, it can look like a mess of brushstrokes and paint. It's only when we stand back to view the piece from a distance that we fully appreciate the brilliant artistry of the masters of Impressionism. For this reason, I encourage my students to embrace imperfection and the painterly look of collage. Up close, fabric collage will have imperfections. But when observed from a distance, a collage quilt becomes a work of art!

Contrast
The Secret Sauce of Collage Quilts

The most important aspect of color theory is understanding how to create contrast. This chart helps to encapsulate the methods for creating contrast: through color, value, and temperature. Contrast can be either subtle or dramatic, and both types of contrast are important to understand and to use in a composition.

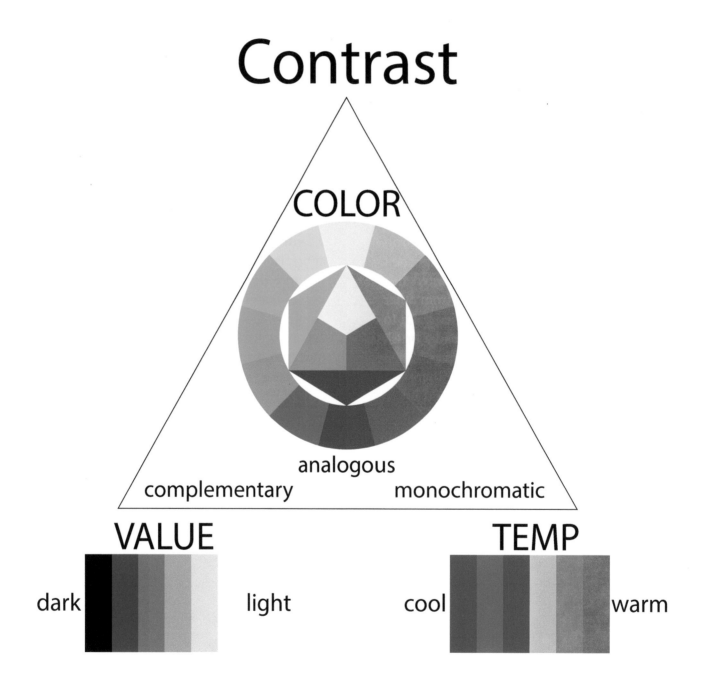

Color

Primary Colors

Red, yellow, and blue are the foundational colors by which all other colors are created.

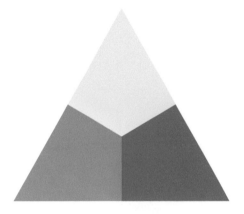

Secondary Colors

Orange, green, and violet are made by mixing primary colors: red and yellow create orange; blue and yellow create green; red and blue create violet.

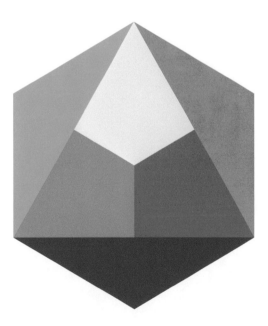

Tertiary Colors

These colors round out the spectrum and are created by the blending of one primary color and one secondary color, as indicated by their names: Blue-Violet, Red-Orange, Yellow-Green, and so on. We also know these colors by such names as vermilion, chartreuse, magenta, periwinkle, teal, etc.

Unlimited Colors

By continuing to mix and blend colors, we see that there really are countless colors! The list of colors and their names is long and sometimes confusing. A single root color, blue, for example, is also known by it's variations by names like cobalt, cerulean, indigo, ultramarine, Prussian blue, etc.

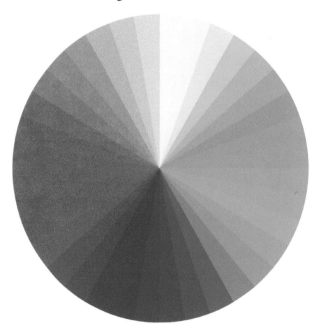

Analogous

This grouping is made from colors next to each other on the color wheel. Analogous colors create subtle contrast. These families can contain just two colors, or can contain several colors.

Teal and Chartreuse

Periwinkle, Cobalt, Ultramarine, Teal, Chartreuse, Green and Emerald

Cinnabar and Saffron

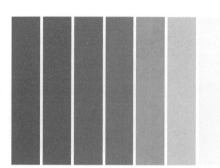

Fuchsia, Pink, Vermilion, Cinnabar, Saffron, Goldenrod and Lemon

Kelly Green and Gamboge

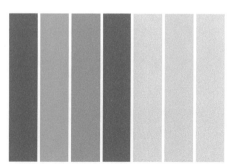

Kelly Green, Teal, Green, Chartreuse, Absinthe, Avocado and Gamboge

11

Complementary

This grouping is made from colors on the opposite side of the color wheel. Complementary colors create dramatic contrast. Think of a spinner that sits in the middle of the color wheel- the spinner will always point out the colors that are complementary to each other.

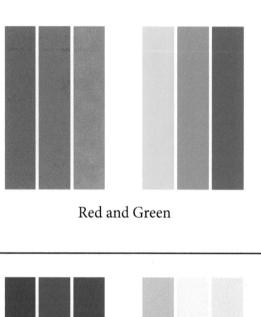

Red and Green

Violet and Yellow

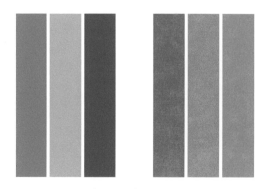

Blue and Orange

Monochromatic

This grouping is made from the same color family in different *values* or *temperature* (more about value and temperature in the next section). Monochromatic color families can be either dramatic or subtle.

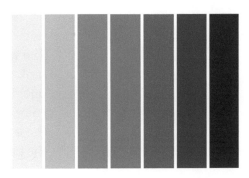

A monochromatic combination can create dramatic contrast when using colors that are far apart on the value spectrum...

... Or the combination can create a subtle contrast when using colors that are close to each other in value or temperature.

Examples of Color Contrast

The vibrant colors of the red and pink flowers in this quilt (**Felicity**) offer a dramatic *complementary* color contrast to the green of the leaves peeking out behind the petals. Likewise, the purple and yellow flowers also follow a complementary color scheme.

The purple colors in this *monochromatic* color scheme run the spectrum from light to dark, and warm to cool.

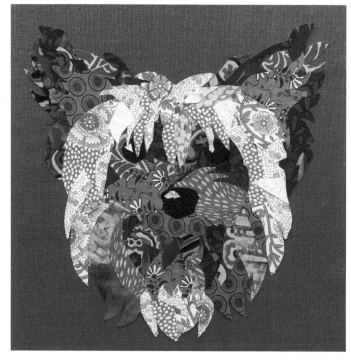

This is a great example of an *analogous* color palette. Purple, blue, and green look stunning together!

The leaves also illustrate an *analogous* palette. Notice the richness and depth of them because of the subtle contrast in color between yellow-green, green, teal, and blue.

Value
The Spectrum of Light to Dark

Artists refer to values as white, black, or any shade of gray in between. Values are devoid of color.

As quilters, we are going to simply say that value is the lightness or darkness of a color. This color wheel helps us to see the change in each color as it transitions from light to dark

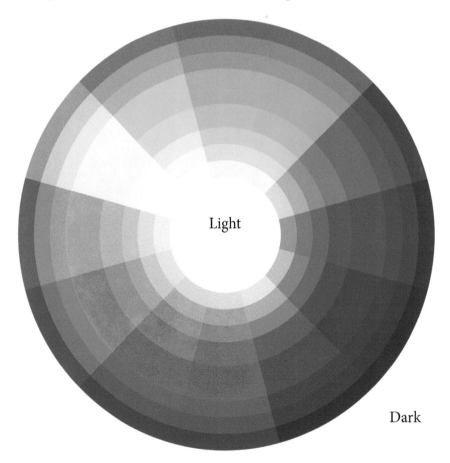

Why Pay Attention to Values?

Variation in value ensures that our design isn't flat, that it has depth and dimension. The interplay between light and dark helps us to understand the shapes and objects in our world. We would still be able to discern the environment around us even if we only saw it in shades of gray.

Furthermore, value helps us to identify things because we are familiar with patterns of light and dark. For example, this bird has a distinctive dark and light pattern that helps us to identify it as a quail. If we mix up the values, or eliminate them entirely, the bird doesn't look right and is more difficult to identify as a quail.

How Do We Discern Value?

It can be very tricky to figure out where on the value spectrum our fabric falls, but don't worry... It's actually NOT important to determine the absolute value of fabric that we are working with! What's critical to understand and to apply in our collage quilts is the concept of relative value.

Value is Relative

One piece of fabric that falls in the middle of the value spectrum can appear lighter or darker based on what is next to it-- that's all we care about when making a collage quilt.

Let's take a random piece of fabric that falls somewhere in the middle of the value spectrum.

When we put it next to a lighter fabric, the original piece looks darker.

If we compare the original piece to a darker fabric, it's easy to see that the original piece looks lighter.

We can create dramatic or subtle contrast depending on which pieces of fabric we are comparing. Do the fabrics we are comparing fall in the mid-tone range of values? If so, they probably have only a subtle amount of contrast between them.

Do the fabrics we are comparing fall on the ends of the spectrum? If so, the contrast between them can be quite dramatic.

Contrast expressed through changes in value can be either subtle or dramatic depending on the degree of difference. Interpreting the degree of contrast is important, and subtle contrast is just as important to see and create as dramatic contrast, because subtle value changes are what help our eye to transition between light and dark areas of a composition.

When trying to create a collage with any degree of realism, the minimum number of values to recognize in a subject is three: light, medium, and dark.

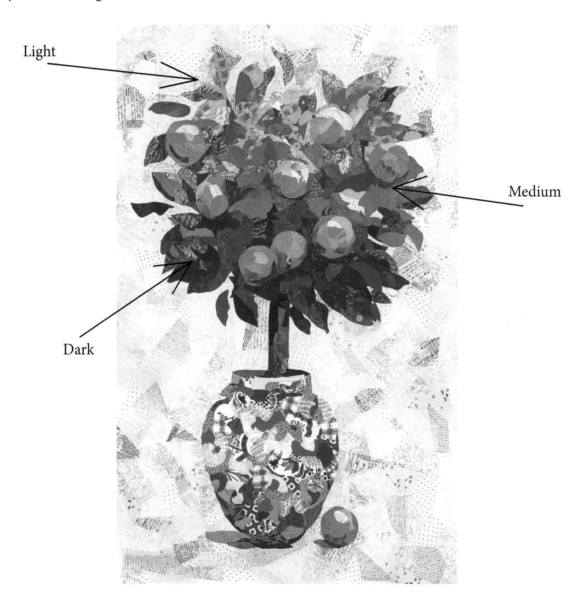

In this project, I focused on just three value changes: light, medium, and dark. You can see this pattern in the topiary, the clementines, and in the pot. Additional subtle variations happen because of the fabric selection (more on that later)!

As the number of values increases, so does the difficulty level of the project. Interpreting six to eight distinct values in a subject is a challenge. But the transitional values between light and dark are what make the subject look more realistic. In *The Horse*, I've tried to interpret six distinct values.

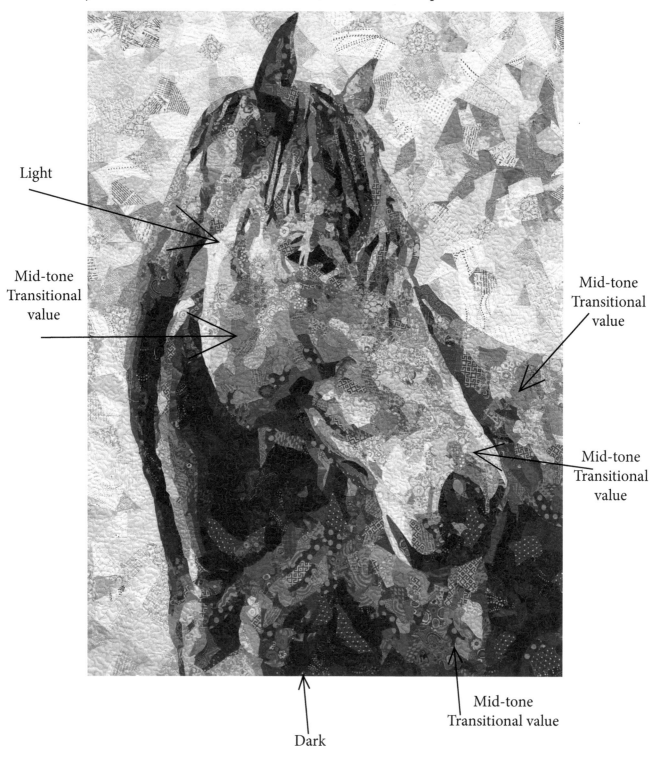

Light

Mid-tone Transitional value

Mid-tone Transitional value

Mid-tone Transitional value

Mid-tone Transitional value

Dark

This collage has five distinct values in the spines of the cactus, which make the plant look dimensional. The pot only has only two value changes, making it look very stylized rather than realistic.

Temperature
The Superpower of Color

Temperature refers to the warmth or coolness of color. We can pretty easily identify the warm and cool colors when we look at the color wheel...

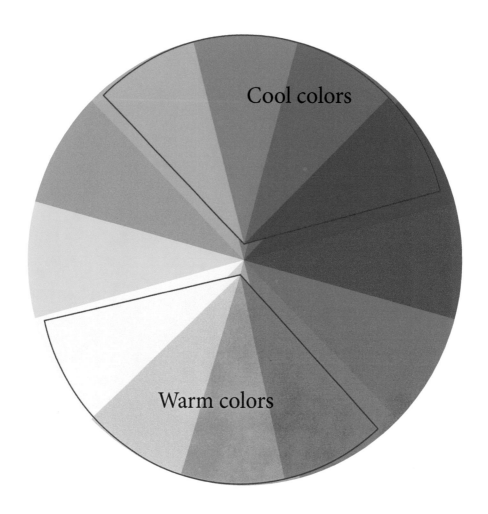

The temperature of color has a psychological effect on us-- it can actually affect our MOOD!

Cool colors are CALMING, QUIET and SUBDUED. Cool colors also recede in a composition, creating depth. A cool color on the walls of a bedroom creates a relaxing environment and can make the room appear larger.

These colors can also cause us to feel melancholy, or a little "blue". A composition dominated by cool colors can be a bit BORING, too.

Conversely, warm colors are EXCITING, DRAMATIC and INTENSE. Warm colors advance in a composition and tend to dominate our attention. Orange, yellow, and red can even cause us to feel alarm, or make us "see red". These colors can also be overwhelming in a composition or on the walls of a room!

Used with permission by the artist, Jane Anne Woodhead

Consider a landscape painting with mountains in the background. What color are they? Generally an artist will use cool colors to convey depth. Mountains are painted blue or purple to create distance on a canvas. In this painting, the artist also used warm colors in the foreground to maximize the depth of the landscape.

In the same way that colors can be expressed in variations of light or dark, each color can be expressed as a warm or cool version of the root color. I like to think of color sliding along a temperature spectrum between warm and cool, the same way we think about a color sliding between light and dark.

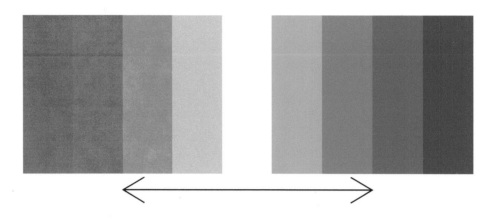

As a color slides toward the orange end of the spectrum, it will appear *warmer*.

As a color slides towards the blue end of the spectrum, it will appear *cooler*.

Every color will have warm and cool versions of itself depending on which direction the color "slides" along the temperature spectrum.

There are warm yellow fabrics that look more orange...

...And cool yellow fabrics that have more of a green cast.

Warm green fabrics that are more olive ...

...And cool green fabrics that lean
towards teal.

Warm purple fabrics that are
muddy and mauve...

..And cool purple fabrics which contain
a lot of blue.

What About Neutrals?

Neutrals are Almost NEVER Neutral.

Generally, we consider grayish or whitish colors to be neutral. However, just like any other color, when we slide gray or white anywhere along the temperature spectrum between warm and cool, they cease to be neutral. To be precise the only truly neutral "colors" are actually VALUES, and not colors at all.

To fully appreciate the idea that neutrals are almost never neutral, swing by a paint store and check out the number of "white" paint chips available! There are hundreds of variations of white-- some are warm, some are cool, some have a yellow undertone, some have a pink tint. You get the idea!

The subtle contrast of warm and cool purple fabrics in this eggplant makes it rich and dimensional, even though the color and value of the veggie is quite consistent (outside of the highlight and shadow areas).

The petals of this flower look interesting and alive because of the subtle contrast of warm and cool red fabrics. The warm red fabrics have a lot of orange in them, while the cool red fabrics appear more pink and purple.

Getting the Temperature Just Right

A good balance of cool colors and warm colors in a composition tends to be the most pleasing. Balance can be an even distribution of warm and cool colors.

Balance can also mean that there is a POP of warm color in a predominantly cool quilt, or a POP of cool in a predominantly warm quilt.

This collage quilt is a good example of how a pop of warm (in the bird's neck area) provides BALANCE to the dominant cool colors used in the majority of the quilt.

Can You Identify Different Types of Contrast?

This quilt, called **Sublime**, is a good example of the three types of contrast: color, value, and temperature. Furthermore, both subtle and dramatic contrast are evident in this quilt.

Dramatic complementary color contrast is the most obvious example of contrast in this quilt (yellow and purple flowers, as well as red flowers and green leaves).

Value contrast is easy to identify in the flowers as they go from dark in the center to light on the outer edges of the petals. Darker values are also used to indicate shadows on the stems that are behind other stems, or beneath flower petals.

Subtle analogous colors can be seen in the leaves and stems of the flowers. The teal, purple, and blue colors in the stems and leaves convey depth and shadow.

Similarly, the *temperature contrast* between the warm yellow-green of the leaves and stems is in contrast to the cool greens, making the overall composition look sun-dappled and lively.

When we place a warm and cool version of the same color next to each other, the effect is an interplay that creates subtle movement and life in the combination.

Creating a collage quilt is entirely different from making a traditional quilt, and the supplies needed are quite different as well. In this section, I'll explain the what, why, and how of supplies you'll need, including fabric selection, methods of adhesion, and tricks for staying organized.

Fabric
How & Why of Selecting What

How Much Fabric?

You'll quickly realize that fabric requirements for collage quilts are very flexible. There are no requirements except to completely cover each section of the quilt as you create the design.

There is NO SUCH THING AS TOO MUCH FABRIC when making a collage quilt.

The greater the variety of fabric we use in each section of the quilt, the more interesting it will be. Variety of fabric will add depth, dimension, and movement in your collage quilts. Because we want a good variety of fabric, we don't need large pieces of fabric. I recommend using scraps from leftover quilt projects, and when you need to purchase fabric, try to buy in 1/8 yard increments.

Using fabric that is 1/8 yard by the width of fabric provides a strip of fabric from which it is very easy to cut a smaller piece. I cut the end of the strip so that I have a piece that is about 4.5" x 6" that can quickly be prepared with fusible web. Then I can neatly fold back up the remaining amount to put away.

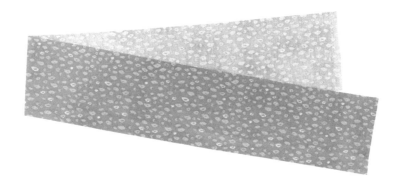

Tip!
Not all fabric shops will cut an 1/8 yard of fabric-- most have minimum requirements of a quarter to half yard. Try to find a fabric shop that will cut any size for you, and be loyal to shops that will provide only what you need.

My shop at CollageQuilter.com sells fabric bundles of one color cut in 1/8 yard strips. Each bundle contains 18 pieces of fabric, in a spectrum of light to dark and warm to cool.

As quilters, the fabric that we tend to buy generally falls in the middle of the value spectrum because it is the most pure color and we have an emotional connection to it. It's rare that we enjoy shopping for fabric that falls on the ends of the spectrum-- the very dark fabrics or the very light fabrics.

However, as collage quilters we quickly learn that we need to "push" the value spectrum of fabric that we use to include the darkest to the lightest values of each color. This requires a conscious effort to shop for fabric outside our comfort zone.

⟵————— "Pushing the Spectrum" to include the —————⟶
darkest and lightest values

When sorting your stash, the following exercise is a good one in helping you to increase the amount of useful fabric in your stash~

1) Select one color and arrange all the pieces of that color from light to dark.
2) Looking at the fabric, ask yourself these questions:
     "Can I push the values in this color by adding light or dark?"
     "Where do I have holes in the spectrum?"
3) Doing this exercise with each color in your stash will help you round out a good palette of fabric for your collage quilt projects!

What Fabric to Use?

Types of Fabric

When shopping for fabric, step outside your comfort zone to select different fabric than what you normally would. For example, if you are crazy about batiks, think about incorporating some interesting prints. If you love bold florals, think about integrating some subtle fabric that reads more like a solid.

Have fun with different textures as well~ use scraps of wool, or ribbon if the idea strikes you!

Batik fabric   Printed fabric

Batik

Batik is a type of fabric that is dyed rather than printed. Batik fabric is generally a more tightly woven fabric than traditional printed quilting cottons. Therefore batiks tends to fray on the edges much less than printed fabrics. Keep this in mind, because we are dealing with LOTS of raw edges in collage quilts. Another thing to keep in mind about batiks-- they are the same (or very similar) on both sides. Batiks offer an immense variety of value and colors. They often "read like a solid" while providing a measure of interest that solid colors don't have.

Printed

Printed fabrics are what give our collage quilts personality and really make them interesting! But dealing with the pattern, scale, and repeat of printed fabrics can be tricky. Don't be afraid to use the big, bold prints that you love-- just keep them in their place-- don't allow them to dominate the quilt. Think about fussy-cutting those bold prints and using them in a unique way. Often I will use the dramatic printed fabric that I love as a source of color inspiration. One strong print can be the color scheme for an entire quilt. Whether you fussy-cut printed fabric or use it to enhance the range of colors in your collage quilt, here are a few things to keep in mind about printed fabrics:
- They fray on the edges more than batiks
- The reverse side of the fabric generally looks different from the front

Tip!

Consider using the reverse side of fabric when you need to "push the value spectrum" of your fabrics. To illustrate, as I was creating my *Adoration* quilt (based on Gustav Klimt's <u>Mother and Child</u> painting), I found it difficult to find a good variety of flesh-colored fabric. I learned that the reverse side of orange and salmon printed fabrics make great light-skin color options!

Because printed fabrics can have such a variety of colors and patterns on them, they can sometimes be problematic for use in collage quilts. Here are some of the challenges when working with printed fabrics:

- The design of the printed fabric can make it difficult to see a dominant color because it features multiple colors
- Relative value is difficult to determine because of high contrast in the design

When shopping for printed fabrics, ask yourself:

1) Can I identify the dominant color in the pattern?
2) Does the design have elements that would be great for fussy-cutting?
3) Will this design be difficult to assign to a value because it is a high contrast print?

There are some fabrics that I rarely purchase because they are difficult to use in a collage quilt. Generally, I stay away from fabric that will stand out too much from surrounding fabric.

These are types of fabric that I don't purchase very often:

- Strong grid patterns like polka dots or stripes
- High contrast designs that use black and white or complementary color schemes
- Novelty fabric that contains images (unless I intend to fussy-cut the images for the collage)
- A pattern with a sparse repeat
- Solid colors

Because we are dealing with a LARGE variety of fabric while making a collage quilt, it's important to have a method for maintaining order. I sort my fabric into 12 colors, so I have 12 containers for scraps and 12 larger containers for folded yardage-- one for each color!

Red • Pink • Yellow • Orange • Green • Blue • Teal
Purple • Gray • White • Brown • Multi-color

Small

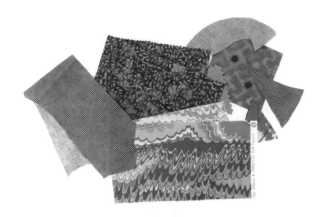 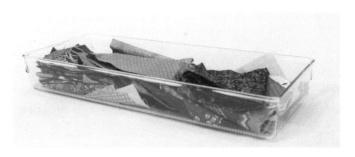

These containers hold cut fabric pieces that are about the size of my palm to pieces that are up to approximately 10". Some of these pieces have fusible web on them and some pieces don't. This is the first size that I go to when I start a new project.

Large

These containers hold folded fabric that ranges in size from 1/8 yard to 1/2 yard . None of the folded fabric has fusible web on it. If I don't find what I'm looking for in my smaller cut pieces of fabric, I will cut a small amount from the folded fabric to work with.

Scissors
The How of Cutting

A great pair of sharp scissors is essential for making collage quilts. I love the Karen K. Buckley 6" perfect scissors. They have a very fine serrated edge that cuts through fabric like butter. In addition, the size of them is easy to wield with smaller pieces of fabric.

Size of Fabric Pieces

You'll be cutting pieces that vary in size and shape, so here's my rule of thumb about the size of pieces:

> Keep fabric pieces smaller than the palm of your
> hand but larger than your thumbnail.

If you are working on a section of the quilt that is large and without much detail, use larger pieces of fabric. When working on a section that requires more precision, cut fabric pieces smaller. Also keep in mind that smaller pieces will allow for a greater variety of fabric!

Detailed areas of the design may require smaller pieces.

Bigger pieces of fabric are good to use in large areas without detail.

Shape

There is no "correct" shape to cut. However, there is an *efficient* way to cut all the pieces you'll be using in your projects.

After you've gathered all the fabric you'll be using in your project, cut the fabric into manageable pieces. Because most of the fabric purchase is 1/8 yard, I can easily cut a rectangle that is about 6"-8" x 4.5"

A triangle from the corner is the fastest and easiest way to cut into the fabric.

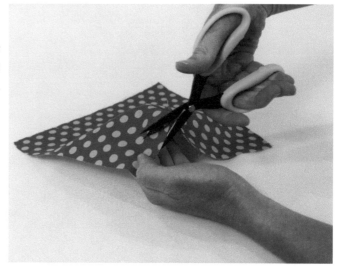

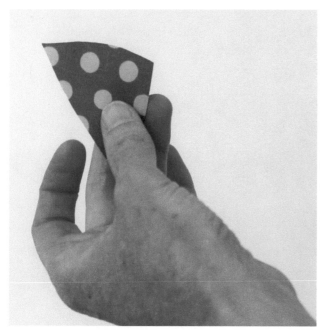

After cutting a triangle, I round one of the edges of the triangle to make it fit along any curved areas of the design.

I only cut as I work-- meaning, I do not cut multiple small pieces at the same time.

Fussy-Cutting

Fussy-cutting is a method of cutting fabric to capture the design or motif in the fabric. In the example below, I've Identified a leaf that I want to use in a collage...

Cutting the leaf away from the fabric gives me an identifiable element to use in my collage projects.

Fussy-cut pieces add an interesting detail
amongst random-cut fabric pieces

Often I will add pieces that are
rounded if it will enhance the
shape of the object

Adhesives

Glue or Fusible Web

Collage quilt-making involves gluing or fusing small pieces of fabric to a foundation. The foundation, or background is also fabric and can be either a solid piece of fabric, pieced, or collaged.

There are distinct differences in adhesive methods and I encourage you to experiment with using glue and fusible web as optional techniques for adhesion so that you can decide which you prefer.

Comparison of Glue & Double-Sided Fusible Web

Water-Soluble Tacky Glue	Permanent Fabric Glue	Double-Sided Fusible Web
•Highest incidence of frayed edges	•Highest incidence of frayed edges	•Least amount of fraying on edges
•Least expensive	•Inexpensive	•Expensive
•Requires pinning pieces prior to adhering	•Requires pinning pieces prior to adhering	•Has convenient temporary stick
•Easy clean-up	•Permanent	•Permanent
•Least stiff	•Messy	•Requires preparation on fabric
		•More stiff than glue

There are advantages and disadvantages with each product. I like the speed and ease of using permanent fabric glue (Fabric Fusion®), but it can be messy!

Although it takes extra time to prepare my fabric with fusible web before I can dig in on a project, this is my preferred method of adhesion-- mostly because the brand that I like (Lite Steam a Seam 2) has a temporary stick that allows me to audition fabric pieces before they are permanently adhered.

> A word about frayed edges~ working with raw edges in a collage quilt can result in frayed edges. Sometimes this is a desirable effect because fraying can result in a soft texture to the quilt. However, if you prefer to minimize fraying, fusible web is the best product to use along with dense quilting. (More info about quilting on page 56).

Water-Soluble Glue (Aleene's Original Tacky Glue®)

- It has a very thick and sticky consistency which requires spreading or smoothing with your fingertip at the edges of each piece of fabric. This makes it a bit more cumbersome to use than Fabric Fusion, and also causes the edges to fray a bit as you spread the glue.

- It dries clear.

- This glue will wash away if you wash the quilt. Therefore, it's possible to remove a piece of fabric that has been glued to the foundation by saturating it with water.

- It's easy to clean up-- just roll between fingers or wash away with soap and water.

- Edges of fabric pieces will fray the most when using this glue.

Permanent Glue (Aleene's Fabric Fusion®)

- It has a thin consistency and is easy to apply to fabric pieces by running a small bead of glue around the edge of each piece.

- While this glue is clear, it dries somewhat shiny. Therefore, don't get it on the front of your quilt or you may notice the sheen.

- Use caution when working with this glue~ it will ruin clothes if it gets on them.

- There is no way to reposition or remove fabric pieces once the glue has dried.

- It is not water soluble, and cleaning it off your fingertips is a little tricky-- wash thoroughly with soap and water and peel it off.

- It allows edges of fabric pieces to fray more than fusible web.

Double-Sided Fusible Web

This is a product designed to be activated by heat and/or steam from your iron and will fuse two pieces of fabric together when sandwiched between them. There are several types and brands of fusible web, but my favorite is Lite Steam a Seam 2®.

Regardless of which fusible web you use, always read the manufacturers directions for use! And keep in mind that using fusible web requires preparation of the fabric prior to getting started on a project.

Tips for Using Lite Steam a Seam 2® (SAS)

- SAS will temporarily stick to the foundation panel, allowing for fabric pieces to be repositioned or removed easily prior to fusing permanently.

- Once applied to a piece of fabric, the SAS on the reverse side of the fabric provides a very thin and consistent layer of adhesive on the entire piece of fabric. This results in a very secure fuse and minimal fraying.

- A finished collage quilt made using SAS is stiffer than a quilt made using glue. To minimize the stiffness, I recommend steaming the finished quilt top excessively to help the glue soften and dissipate the temporary layers of adhesive.

- I don't recommend storing fabric with SAS on it, because the product makes fabric difficult to fold. This is one of the reasons that I have two sizes of fabric-- those smaller scraps that have fusible on them are kept loose, while the larger pieces that are folded, do not.

- My "Parchment Pressing" method *only* works with SAS.

- Lite Steam a Seam2 comes in sheets or rolls. Because I use a large amount of SAS, I prefer to acquire a large roll at a time.

Sundry Supplies

Parchment Paper

Parchment paper, also known as baking paper, is a product that I like to use for some collage projects.

Parchment paper is an inexpensive, heat-resistant, non-stick surface onto which I can create each element of a design independently before I create the final composition of the quilt. Each element then acts like a sticker--it can be peeled away from the parchment paper in one piece and applied to a foundation fabric. This gives me complete control over the size and composition of my project!

Fabric must be prepared with Lite Steam a Seam 2 in order for this technique to work.

> I prefer to purchase Parchment Paper that is 18" wide. If you cannot find paper in that width, you can tape two pieces together at the seam with masking tape.

Foam Core Covered in Felt

1/4" foam core can be found in large sheets at most craft stores in a standard size of 40" x 32". You can have it cut to a smaller size if your space doesn't allow for the full size. Staple or tape felt to the board to create a working surface. The felt ensures that the foundation fabric doesn't slip around, and protects the foam core from the heat of an iron. The foam enables you pin fabric pieces to the design.

Pins

When using glue as the method of adhesion, pins are essential. Use pins to hold pieces of fabric in place on a section of the collage quilt as a way to "audition" fabric choices. I also use pins to score the paper on fabric that has Steam a Seam on it.

Pointed Tweezers

These tweezers are helpful when applying or replacing fabric pieces from a work in progress.

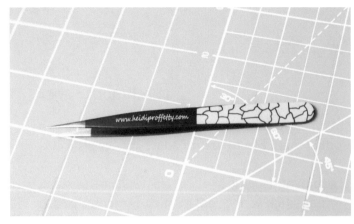

Mini Iron

When using the "Parchment Pressing" method, having a mini iron at your fingertips is extremely helpful. These are two varieties of irons that I use in my studio. The wand iron on the right is great for ironing small pieces to the parchment paper because I can wield it with more control.

The iron on the left is handy for pressing scraps of fabric as I need to without leaving my work station.

In addition to having a small iron nearby, a 1/2" wool pressing mat is practically essential for use with a small iron.

Tables

Folding tables are helpful to set fabric and other supplies on as you work. I also like using a drafting table for larger projects because I can see the whole piece as I work. I set my foam core on the drafting table.

THE FOUNDATION METHOD

3

With the right tools, and by applying principles of color theory to the process, we are ensured success in making a beautiful collage quilt!

The foundation method means that fabric pieces will be applied directly to a whole cloth panel that has the design either traced or printed on it. Using the foundation method for making a collage quilt means that the composition of the design has already been created according to the pattern, therefore the size of the quilt is unchangeable.

The process for creating a collage quilt using a foundation panel follows four basic steps:
Prepare the Design,
Select & Prepare Fabric,
Collage
Finish.

The easiest foundation designs are those which have the design preprinted in shades of gray on white cotton. A preprinted foundation eliminates the need to trace the design, and the only preparation required to begin is to press the panel that comes in the package. (Many of the patterns sold on my website contain a preprinted design).

An alternative to purchasing a preprinted pattern is to trace the design onto a piece of thin white cotton. When preparing your own foundation, trace just the outline of each value change, and keep the template handy to see where value changes should occur.

When I'm working on a foundation panel design, I like to have my work surface (foam core covered in felt) set up at an angle on my drafting table. This makes it easier to see the entire design at one time.

Plum Pretty

Step ONE

Prepare the Design

Have the image from this book, found in the appendix, enlarged to any size you'd like your finished project to be. I have enlarged it by 375% and printed it at an office store on 24" x 36" paper.

Trace the enlarged design onto foundation fabric using a light box or by hanging the design in a window. In the example of **Plum Pretty** I use a 24" x 36" piece of white cotton fabric for the foundation.

When tracing the design, be sure to outline each section that has a separate value. In **Plum Pretty**, there are 3 distinct values in the plums, so be sure to trace those areas. I use a pen to trace, but you can use a pencil. All the tracing marks will eventually be covered by fabric. The leaves of the stem have only one value, which makes this design easy to trace!

50

Select & Prepare Fabric

Gather a wide variety of fabric in the colors you have chosen for the design. Each gray section of the design will represent a value change, and will require multiple pieces of fabric which represent that value.

For example, in **Plum Pretty**, the plums have distinct gray values representing the highlight, main, and shadow areas. Therefore, I will select a "set" of fabric for each section.

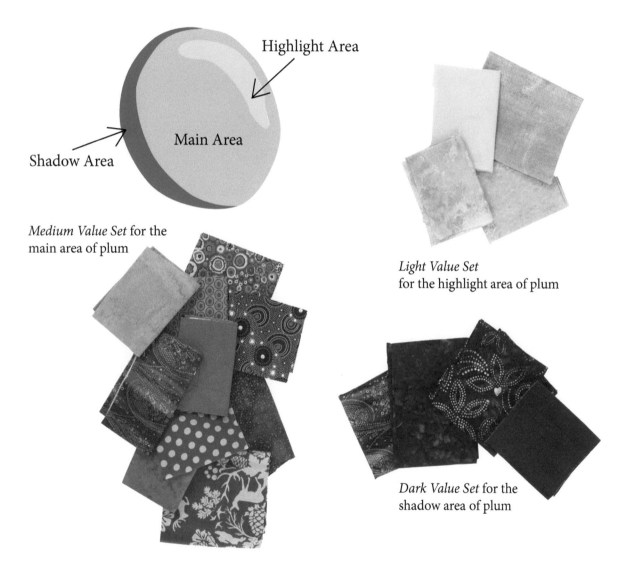

Highlight Area

Main Area

Shadow Area

Medium Value Set for the main area of plum

Light Value Set for the highlight area of plum

Dark Value Set for the shadow area of plum

Gather fabric for the branches and the blossoms in the same way as outlined for the selection of leaves and the plums. Once you have selected fabric for the project, you will need to decide whether to use glue or fusible web to adhere the fabric to the foundation.

If you select glue, as I chose to do for this project, you can move forward to step three. If you'd prefer to use a fusible, now is the time to prepare all your fabric with the fusible.

Step THREE

Collage

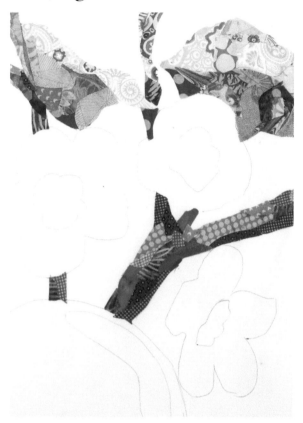

Choose where to begin on the design-- either the darkest or lightest value in the design OR the area that would be behind other elements of the design. With the **Plum Pretty** design, I begin with the stem and leaves because they are behind the blossoms and plums.

Begin cutting pieces and pinning them to the area of the design you are working on. Ensure that each piece overlaps those around it-- never butt the pieces up next to each other. (Overlap pieces by 1/4" -1/2" depending on shapes).

After I am pleased with the fabric placement, I adhere the fabric pieces to the foundation with glue.

When using Lite Steam a Seam 2® fusible web (SAS), pins are not necessary-- simply score the paper on the back of the fabric pieces with a pin and peel away the paper to expose the adhesive. Finger press each fabric piece to the foundation panel. The fabric pieces are only temporarily applied to the foundation and will fall off if you move the project around. Therefore, when you have finished a section of the collage, press and steam it to permanently fuse it to the foundation fabric.

Work in sections or "chunks" of the quilt, rather than focusing on the entire quilt at the same time.

The leaves in the design are all the same value, yet we know that leaves have multiple light and dark patterns on them. I decide to employ a little TRICK... I broaden the spectrum of values for the leaves, but I won't worry about the placement of fabric very much. Instead, I *let the fabric do the work*! Letting the fabric do the work means trusting that an interesting combination of fabric will create something spectacular that I wouldn't have come up with if I were just thinking, "green leaf."

This is the fun of making a collage quilt, and it's also where we can apply our knowledge of color theory to make an amazing one of a kind art quilt! Play with the fabric! Be brave and step outside your comfort zone-- I promise you'll be pleasantly surprised at how the temperature and value changes create dimension and vibrancy.

How Much Should I Overlap when Applying Pieces?

Make sure that fabric pieces overlap by a minimum of 1/4". But because pieces will vary in shape and size, it's alright if the overlap is up to an inch or more. Just make certain that the pieces overlap enough that the traced design on the foundation fabric is covered completely. Overlap ensures that fabric shrinkage which occurs with quilting or washing will not expose the foundation fabric.

Considering the Background

Leaving the background white is the easiest option and one that provides high contrast between the collaged area of the quilt and the negative space of the background. This is what I choose to do for the **Plum Pretty** quilt.

An alternative to leaving the negative space of the collage white is to cut away the foundation fabric and apply the collaged section to a different background. This is more difficult with designs like **Plum Pretty** that have intricate shapes, but works well with designs like **Cactus.**

After cutting the foundation fabric away, simply apply permanent fabric glue to the edges of the back side of the collage and adhere it to either a pieced or solid background.

Edge-to-Edge Collage

Another option for the background of a foundation collage quilt is to collage it from edge-to-edge so that the entire foundation is covered.

This method requires some forethought before beginning the collage to ensure that the entire palette, including background fabric, is harmonious. Edge-to-edge collage creates a very artistic and consistent look. The ***June Bloom*** design is a quilt that has edge-to-edge collage.

Finish

Once the entire collage quilt top is completed it's time to quilt! Make a "quilt sandwich" with the collaged quilt top, batting and backing, just as with a traditional quilt.

The quilting design can be an all-over edge to edge design or custom free-motion quilting. It is not necessary to stitch around the edge of each piece, but dense quilting is essential to ensure that each raw-edged piece of fabric is tacked down securely. Distance between stitching lines should be no more that 1/2".

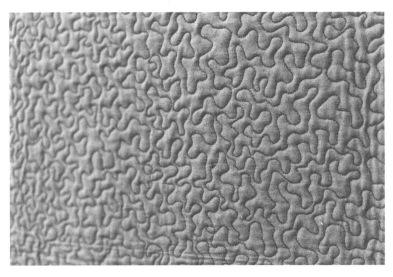

Edge to Edge Stipple Quilting

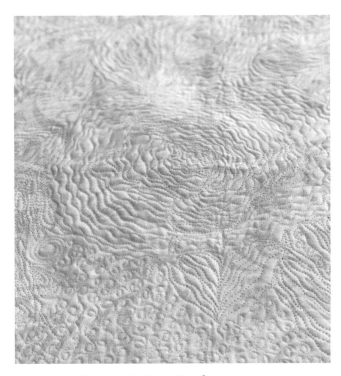

Needles

Always be sure to use a sharp needle! Titanium needles are especially good for collage quilts because they resist breaking and bending. Also, non-stick needles (designed with an anti-adhesive or Teflon coating) are perfect for using when quilting a collage quilt.

The use of a non-stick needle will minimize residue on the needle of your machine. But to clean any residue that does accumulate, simply wipe the needle with a cotton ball saturated in rubbing alcohol.

Custom Free-Motion Quilting

Thread

I prefer to use 100% polyester thread that is 100#. This is very fine, thin, thread with less chance of breaking because it's polyester. Superior Threads makes a version called Microquilter thread that I like.

Plum Pretty
24" x 36"

I select a contrasting fabric to apply a continuous binding once the quilting is complete.

Art in Bloom

Art in Bloom
24" x 24"

Prepare the Design

Take this book to a copy store to have the image enlarged and printed at the size you'd like (template is in the appendix of this book). Trace the enlarged version of the design onto lightweight white cotton using a light box or by hanging the design in a window.

When tracing the design, be sure to outline each section that has a separate value. I use a pen to trace, but you can use a pencil. All the tracing marks will eventually be covered by fabric.

Alternatively, you can purchase the pattern from my website. The pattern contains a foundation panel with the design preprinted-printed on it so no tracing is required.

Use the link below to get a 30% discount on the purchase of the pattern (discount will be automatically applied at checkout):

Point your smart phone camera at this code...
It will automatically provide a link in your
phone browser to the CollageQuilter.com
website.

Select and Prepare Fabric

Once the design is either traced onto fabric or you've purchased the preprinted-printed foundation panel, you are ready to begin selecting and preparing fabric!

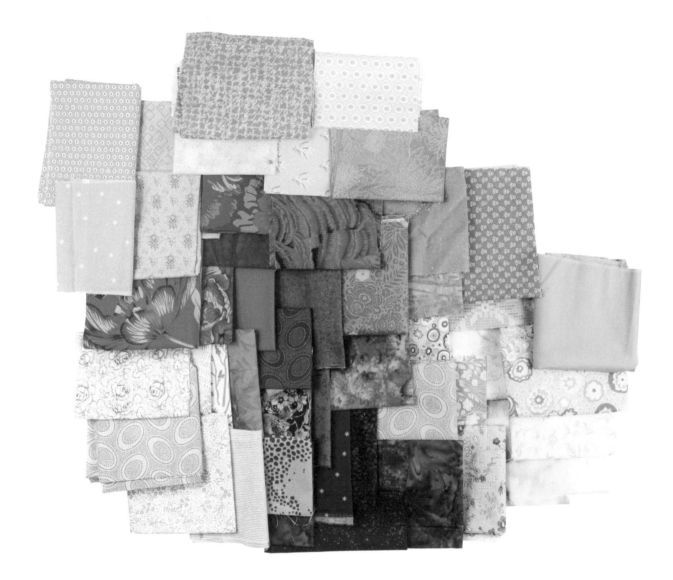

Here is the assortment of fabric I selected for the main elements of the design(excluding the gray fabric I selected for the background). My choice of fabric includes a wide variety of pinks for the flowers, greens for the leaves and blues for the pot. Each color contains a spectrum from light to dark, along with variations in temperature.

At this stage in the process, it's good to pull together more fabric than you think you'll need.

More fabric = more fun!

Sorting According to Value

I can see that there are four shades of gray in the greenery of the floral arrangement. Therefore, I separate my green fabric into four value "sets" or groups: dark, medium-dark, medium, and light.

I sort the other colors I'll be using in the collage the same way.

Preparing Fabric with Fusible Web

For this project, I will be using Lite Steam a Seam 2® (SAS). After I have selected the fabric that I intend to use in a collage project, I prepare each piece with fusible. To do this, I start out with pieces of fabric that are about 6" - 10" wide by 4.5" high (Remember that 4.5" is the height of fabric if you purchase 1/8 yard). I will place the fabric on the exposed adhesive (wrong side of fabric to the adhesive). Lightly iron the adhesive to the fabric.

Collage

Where Should I Begin?

The answer to this question is dependent upon the design of the quilt, but here are my recommendations: in a quilt like *Art in Bloom*, I recommend starting with the background or area of the design that would appear to be behind or underneath foreground elements. It can also be a good idea to consider starting with the darkest or lightest area of the design. Approaching a collage quilt this way helps to establish the value contrast that will define the subject.

However, I'm notorious for breaking my own rules and the end result turns out just fine-- even if I've made it harder for myself by starting with foreground elements. The actual order of layering does not matter in the end. One example of this is the *Sublime* quilt. I completed all the flowers and leaves and intended to leave the background white.

However, after I had finished it I wanted to do something more interesting in the background, and decided to collage it. You would never know that the background was completed last!

With other quilt designs, like *The Horse* or *Grizzly*, I also completed the background last. I'm glad that I did so that my labor on the main focus of the quilt was not subject to what I might have done in the background. With *The Horse*, I had envisioned a dark, moody background. But I would have limited myself in selecting the colors of the horse, had I done the background as I originally envisioned. As it turned out, I re-worked the background three times before I was satisfied with the color scheme of the quilt.

I begin applying pieces of fabric to the foundation panel by cutting a small piece from a rectangle of fabric that has been prepared with Lite Steam a Seam 2 (SAS). Starting on the gray background, I score the paper covering the SAS, to easily peel the paper away and expose the sticky surface on the back of the fabric. I finger press each piece to the foundation fabric, ensuring that each piece overlaps those around it slightly (anything from 1/8" to 1/2" is an appropriate amount of overlap).

The size of each shape is between the size of the palm of my hand and my fingernail. The shape of each piece is quite random.

I continue to apply pieces of fabric to the foundation panel, using the gray tones in the design as a guide for value changes and fabric placement.

It becomes a little bit like a paint-by-number project, except that we are using fabric instead of paint!

In addition to following the values in the design, I have fun with the design by applying my understanding of where light and shadows may fall in the still life design. You can see that by using darker fabric on these leaves, the leaves look like they might be in shadow as they protrude from the bouquet. Similarly, the darker fabric towards the top of the pot suggests that there is a shadow being cast from the overhanging greenery.

I also enjoy fussy-cutting pieces of fabric, as you can see in the center of this large pink flower.

My collage is complete after the entire foundation panel is covered with fabric, and when I'm satisfied with the design! Using Lite Steam a Seam 2 allows all the pieces to stick temporarily to the foundation panel. I can still remove and replace any of the fabric pieces that aren't quite right until I press the entire collage.

Step FOUR

Finish

When I'm pleased with the composition, I will press the finished design with a HOT, STEAMY iron. The steam is especially important because it will help the temporary layers of adhesive to dissipate and activate the permanent fusible.

There is more than one way to display your work, and for this project, I decided that I'd like to frame it in a unique way to highlight the handmade nature of the piece. The piece is "floating" between the glass of the frame.

There is more than one way to display your work, and for this project, I decide that I'd like to frame it in a unique way to highlight the hand-made nature of the piece. The piece is "floating" between the glass of the frame.

4
THE PARCHMENT
PRESSING METHOD

When creating a project using the parchment pressing method, the individual elements of the final design will be constructed on parchment paper first, and then peeled off like a sticker to be adhered to a background fabric.

The Parchment Pressing method allows for creative control over the composition of the design and the overall size of the quilt. Employing this method for making a collage quilt requires the use of parchment paper (as the name suggests).

Just like making a collage quilt using the foundation method, there are four steps in the process of making a parchment pressing collage quilt:

Prepare the Design,
Select & Prepare Fabric,
Collage
Finish.

Tea Party

Prepare the Design

To prepare the design when creating a Parchment Pressing project, enlarge the designs from the book found in the appendix to the indicated size (or whatever size you choose). Cut a piece of parchment paper that will cover the design you are working on. Remember that with this method, you'll create each piece of the design independently.

Trace the design onto the parchment paper using a light box if you have one. If you don't have a light box, trace it by hanging it up in a light window.

Select Color Palette & Prepare Fabric

There is no need to select all the fabric for each element at the outset, but it is important to decide on the overall color scheme.

I have selected pastel versions of pink, blue, green, yellow, and teal for my tea party quilt.

Once I have selected the color scheme for the entire quilt, I need to select the fabrics for each teapot or teacup.

I decide that one of these teapots will be teal. I make certain to include lights, mediums and darks.

For this teapot, I have selected over two dozen fabrics
~ the more the merrier!

Once I've chosen the fabric, I cut it to a manageable size-- about 6" x 4.5", and then prepare it with Lite Steam a Seam 2.

Once my fabric is selected and prepared, I can begin to collage the first element.

I'll go through this process of fabric selection and preparation for each element that is a different color.

Step THREE

Collage

I begin the collage by cutting pieces from my selected fabric that are triangles or rectangles. Often, I will soften the hard angles of a cut of fabric by rounding one of the edges.

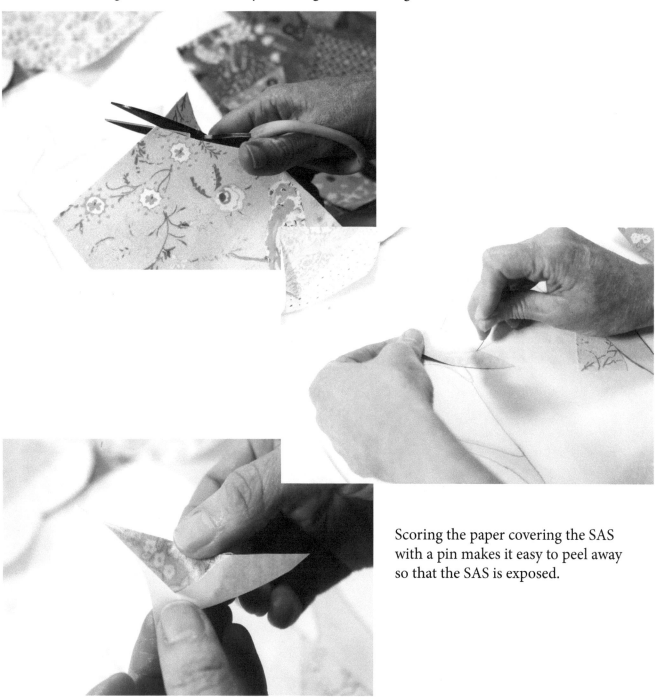

Scoring the paper covering the SAS with a pin makes it easy to peel away so that the SAS is exposed.

Applying fabric to parchment paper is a little different than applying fabric to a foundation panel. Parchment paper is a non-stick surface, and often the first few pieces applied to the parchment paper won't stick very well. It's helpful to use a hot wand iron to press the first few pieces to the parchment paper-- this will activate the adhesive so that it sticks. Subsequent pieces will adhere temporarily to the surrounding pieces of fabric.

Apply fabric pieces following the gray-tone guide, matching the relative value of fabric. As the value on the template gets darker, use the darker fabric. In lighter areas of the design use lighter fabric, and so forth.

The size of fabric pieces will vary depending on the size of the area to be covered, and as the design gets smaller or more intricate, the size of each piece should be smaller as well.

I like to keep my Parchment Pressing projects flat while I'm working on them. The individual elements made using the parchment pressing method tend to be smaller projects, and the fabric pieces don't stick to the parchment paper as well as they do a foundation panel. Keeping the work surface flat reduces the chance that fabric pieces will fall off as I'm working.

You can either leave the design underneath the parchment paper so that you can see changes in gradient, or pin it next to the parchment paper with the tracing so that you can refer to it easily.

Continue to apply fabric pieces to the parchment paper. It's easy to remove or replace any of the fabric pieces at this stage using pointed tweezers or a pin.

When satisfied with the finished element, press the design with a hot iron while it's still on the parchment paper to ensure that all the fabric pieces are adhered to one another. Don't use steam at this point!

Leave the element secured to the parchment paper until you are ready to work on the final composition.

Make as many teacups and teapots as you'll need for your own

Tea Party!

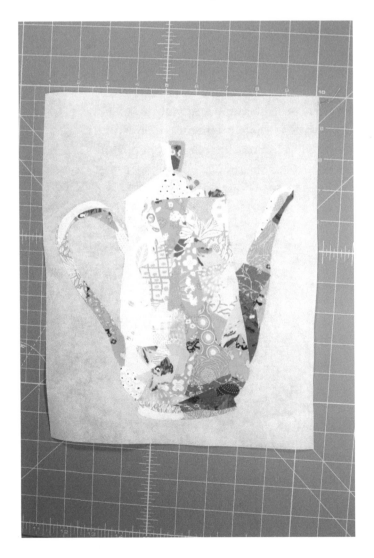

Tip!
Create the reverse version of the pots and cups by flipping the template over and tracing onto the parchment paper from the wrong side of the template!

Step FOUR

Finish

Making Blocks

When each collage is complete, it's time to create the blocks for the quilt. With the Tea Party quilt, I've decided to add the collaged teapots and teacups to wonky log cabin blocks to further emphasize the whimsy of the tea party theme.

To create the wonky log cabin blocks, follow these steps:

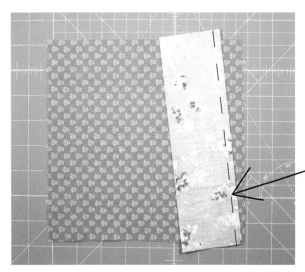

1) Select the background fabric for each teapot and teacup. Cut a square or rectangle of that fabric, then cut a strip of coordinating fabric to begin building the block. Line up the strip at an angle and stitch along the edge of the strip.

2) Sew right sides together along this edge with a 1/4" seam.

3) After sewing the pieces together, trim the excess and press the seam open.

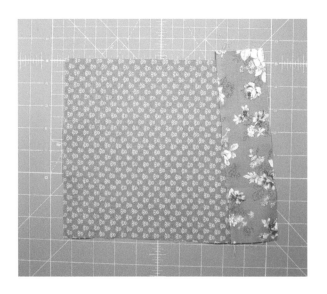

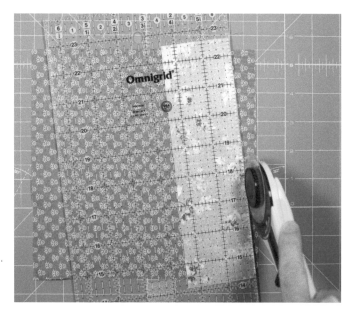

74

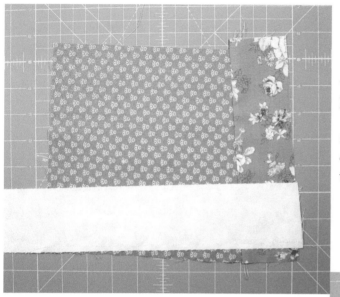

4) Select the next few pieces of fabric that complement the color scheme.

5) Prior to applying the next strip of coordinating fabric, straighten the edge by trimming again.

Repeat these steps with subsequent fabric pieces, until the block becomes large enough that it can be trimmed to 16.5" square, (or whatever size you'd like your blocks to be).

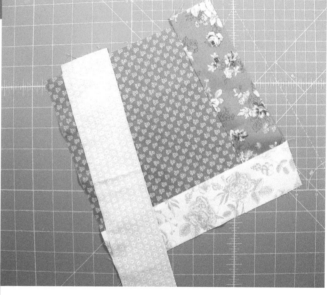

Strips of fabric can be any width, and can even be pieced together. The only requirement is to ensure the length is longer than the edge of the block-- this will require longer strips of fabric as the block grows in size.

When the quilt blocks are complete, peel each collage away from the parchment paper and apply them to the blocks. Press with a hot, steamy iron to permanently fuse the collage to the fabric in the blocks.

Using a 1/4" seam, sew the blocks together to create the quilt! Make the quilt as large or small as you'd like, depending on the number of blocks you create.

Quilting & Binding

My favorite way to finish a quilt is to ship it off to my long-arm quilter, as I did with the Tea Party quilt! A visit to your local quilt shop may put you in touch with people who offer long-arm quilting for hire.

After the quilting is finished, put a continuous binding on and it's ready to use!

Can I Wash a Collage Quilt?

Generally, a collage quilt is considered an art quilt, and not used as a bed quilt. However, if you keep in mind that the raw-edged pieces used in the quilt will fray a bit, there is nothing stopping you from washing the quilt.

The keys to ensure the quilt washes up nicely are: 1) Dense quilting so that each piece is secure. 2) Permanent glue or fusible is permanent and will withstand washing, but water-soluble glue will wash away with washing. 3) Wash on delicate.

Washing a collage quilt softens it noticeably! But washing will also create wear and tear on the quilt that it won't receive if it's just hanging on a wall.

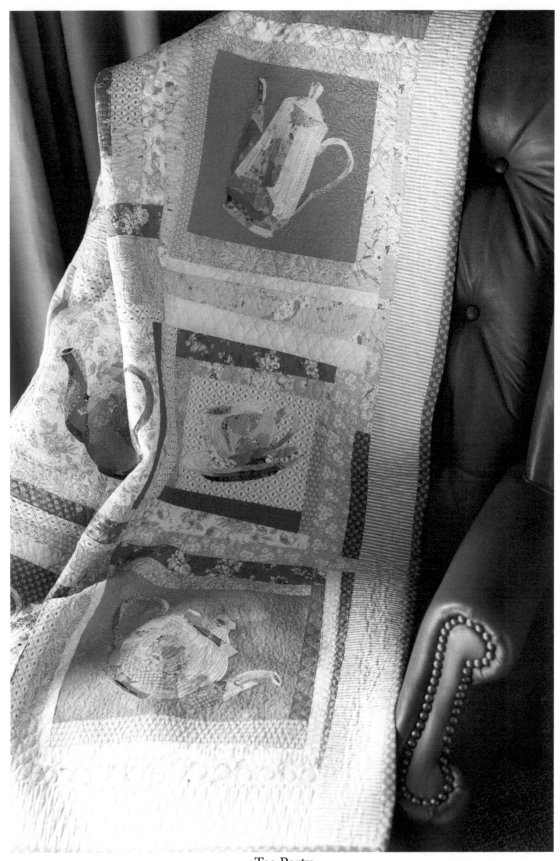

Tea Party
69" x 52"

Pretty Parrots

The parrot patterns, like the teacups and teapots, are Parchment Pressing patterns, and the steps for making them are exactly the same. The parrots are a slightly more advanced project because the birds are multi-colored.

Step ONE

Prepare the Design

Enlarge the parrot designs in the book to the size indicated on the template. My parrots both measure about 19" tall.

Trace the enlarged design onto parchment paper, and pin in place on your work surface.

Select & Prepare Fabric

There are many varieties of Macaw, and each variety has distinctive coloring. After looking at images of these beautiful birds, I decided that the coloring of my parrots will be similar to that of a Military Macaw or a Red-Shouldered Macaw. But you could also use the parrot designs in this book to create a Scarlet Macaw, Hyacinth Macaw, Blue and Yellow Macaw, or a Red and Green Macaw... You get the idea! The coloring for your birds is entirely up to you.

After choosing the coloring for the bird, I select a wide assortment of green and red fabric for the body of the bird, as well as the fabric for his face, and claws. I prepare the fabric by cutting it into manageable rectangles and preparing it with Lite Steam a Seam 2.

Step THREE

Collage

I sort the green and red fabric into a spectrum from light to dark and then begin to apply fabric pieces to the bird following the template-- placing lighter fabric where the gray guide indicates a lighter value, and darker fabric where the gray guide indicates a darker value.

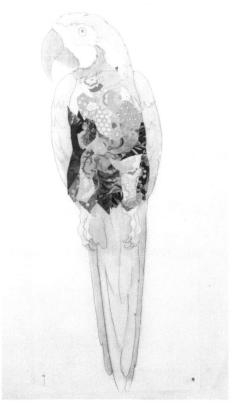

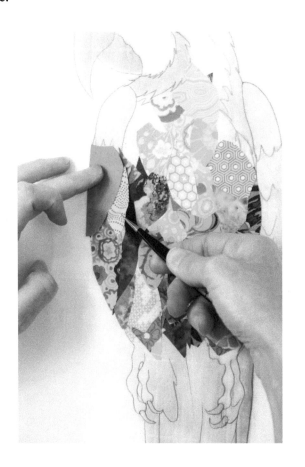

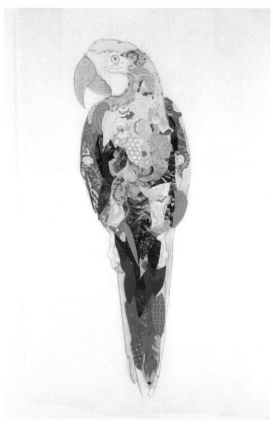

SAS Tracing

To make the eye of the bird, I use a technique called SAS tracing. Here is how to do it:

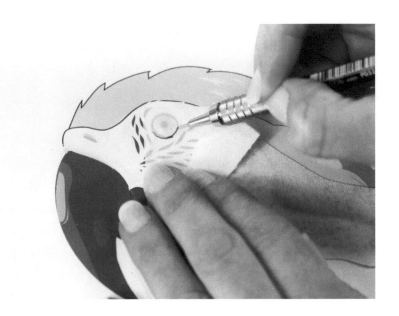

1) Peel the paper away from the back of the selected fabric and trace the eye using a pencil on the paper. Make sure the tracing is on the "inside" of the paper.

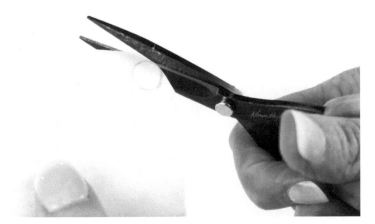

2) Replace the paper covering the SAS on the back side of the fabric. You'll be able to see the tracing through the paper. Follow the tracing to cut out the iris of the eye.

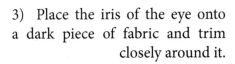

3) Place the iris of the eye onto a dark piece of fabric and trim closely around it.

4) Repeat the first two steps to create a pupil. Layer the pupil onto the eye using tweezers. Press the layers of the eye with a hot iron to fuse them together. Now the eye is ready to apply to the face of the bird!

Using Inktense Pencils

An easy trick to define the claws of the parrot is to draw on them using Inktense pencils.
(This method can be used for any fine detail on the bird~ like on the feathers or the eye, for example).

These pencils are a bit like traditional colored pencils. However, by adding a small amount of water to the pencil drawing using a fine paint brush, it turns into permanent ink!

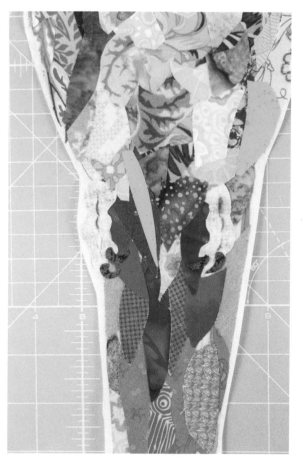

When I have completed the collage of the bird, I press the collage to the parchment paper using a hot, dry iron (no steam, yet).

The collage can be peeled away from the parchment paper in one piece, like a sticker (I love this part)! The back side will have the fusible web on it. Now it can be applied to the background fabric of my choice.

Press the bird onto the background fabric with a hot, steamy iron to secure it permanently.

After applying the parrot on my selected background fabric, I decide to fill in the background with additional leaves to make the background more interesting. This involves creating leaves and stems as I go and fussy-cutting fabric with beautiful leaf patterns. This free-form collage technique doesn't require a template or pattern. It only requires imagination and fabric!

Step FOUR

Finish

When the composition is finished, I press the entire piece. I have selected not to quilt this project, but to create a pair of wall hangings that can be mounted on foam core and hung with removable Velcro strips (Command Strips®).

To finish the parrots as I've done, follow these steps...

1) Add a 1.5" border in selected fabric to the edges of the design.

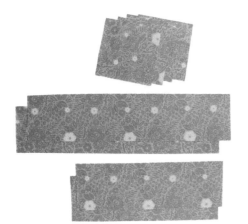

2) Cut four 5" squares and four 4" strips of fabric that are the length of each side. Fold squares with wrong sides together to create triangles, and fold strips of fabric wrong sides together to create 2" strips.

3) Line up the triangles with the corners on the front. Align the raw edge of the strips along each edge of the design (on top of the triangles). Cut the ends of each strip to be about 2" from the corners. (This will make the strips about 4" shorter than the edges of the design).

4) Using a 1/4" seam, sew along the length of each edge to secure triangles and facing strips to the front of the design.

5) Secure the corners by sewing a 45°, then trim the corners to reduce bulk when turned.

6) Flip the facing to the back of the design and press. Secure strips of fabric to the back of the design with fusible web. Leave the corners open to hold the foam core.

Purchase a piece of 1/4" foam core cut 1/2" smaller than the finished design. (Most craft and framing stores carry 1/4" foam core and will cut it to the size you need). Slip the foam core into the corner pockets and use removable Velcro strips to hang the artwork!

Polly the Parrot
16" x 23"

Penny the Parrot
16" x 23"

APPENDIX

Copyright Release

The following designs are for the purpose of copying and are intended for personal use only. They are not to be reproduced for any other purpose. If artwork derived from these designs is entered in art or quilt shows, please indicate that the pattern originates with me, Emily Taylor.

If you'd prefer to download PDFs of the full size templates, scan the QR codes provided with each design.

Full Size of Each Design

Round Teapot   11" x 7.75"

Dainty Teapot   8" x 9.25"

Teacup   8" x 4.75"

Stacked Teacups 7.5" x 7"

Art in Bloom   24" x 24"

Polly Parrot 9" x 19"

Penny Parrot 6" x 18"

(Please note that discrepancies with printer settings may slightly alter the final output size)

Plum Pretty
Enlarge this pattern
up to 375%
Or Scan this code to
access the full size PDF
file to send to print shop.

Art in Bloom
Enlarge by 320% to print on 24" x 36" paper

Or scan this code to purchase the preprinted-printed foundation panel from CollageQuilter.com (30% discount applied at
checkout when using this link)

Penny the Parrot
Enlarge 195% to print on 18" x 24"
paper

Or Scan this code to access the full
size PDF file to send to print shop.

93

Polly the Parrot
Enlarge 195% to print on 18" x 24" paper

Or Scan this code to access the full size PDF
file to send to print shop.

Round Teapot
Enlarge 125% to print on 11" x 17" paper

Or Scan the code to access the
full size PDF file to send to
print shop.

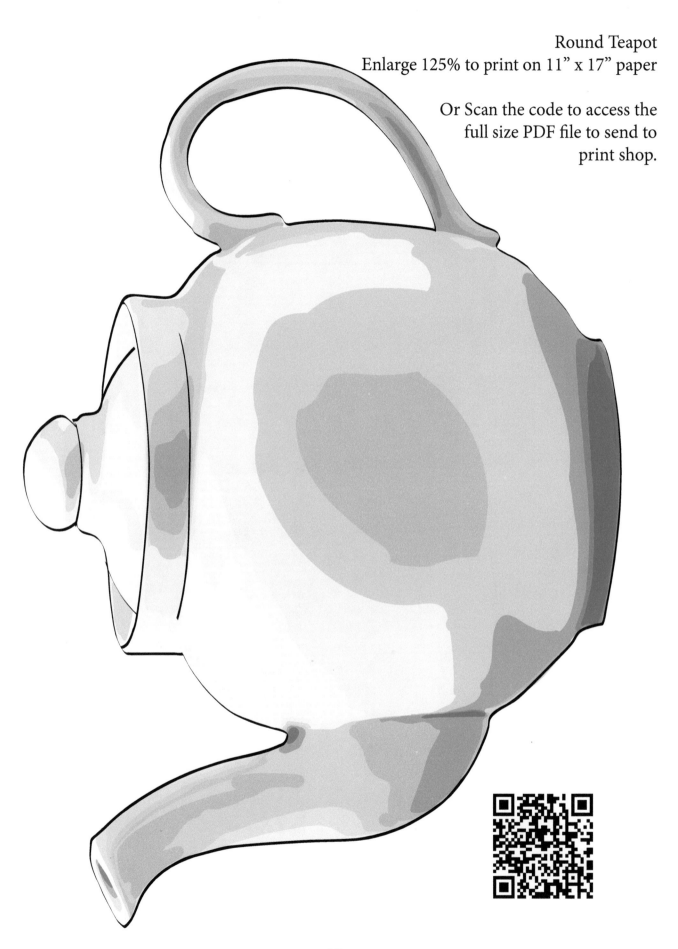

Dainty Teapot
Enlarge 125% to print on 11" x 17"
paper

Or Scan the code to access the full size
PDF file to send to print shop.

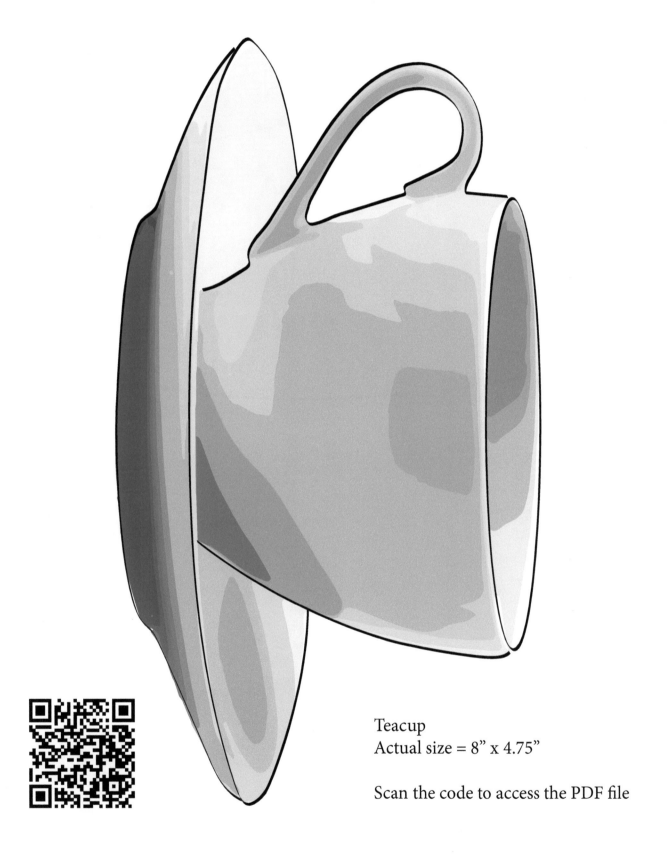

Teacup
Actual size = 8" x 4.75"

Scan the code to access the PDF file

Stacked Teacups
Actual size = 7.5" x 7"

Scan the code to access the PDF file

Additional Resources

CollageQuilter.com

Patterns, fabric, supplies, tutorials

Index of Quilts

INDEX

About the Author
The Collage Quilter

Emily Taylor is a self-taught artist, fabric designer, and quilter. She has been a creative entrepreneur in both the home decor industry and quilt industry for 20+ years. Emily teaches collage quilt workshops online and across the United States.

Emily is an avid outdoor thrill seeker and loves to ski, mountain bike and hike with her husband and three children near their home in Sandy, Utah.

See more of Emily's work or contact her at
CollageQuilter.com

CPSIA information can be obtained
at www.ICGtesting.com
Printed in the USA
BVHW061021051121
620753BV00001B/2